Garden flowers

F. A. Boddy

Pocket Gardener

Sampson Low

Published 1977 by Sampson Low,
Berkshire House, Queen Street, Maidenhead,
Berkshire SL6 1NF
Designed and produced for Sampson Low by
Intercontinental Book Productions
Copyright © 1977 Intercontinental Book Productions
and Floraprint Limited, Nottingham

SBN 562 00075 5

Design by Design Practitioners Limited

Photographs supplied by Floraprint Limited (copyright
I.G.A.), Leslie Johns and Associates, Harry Smith, W.
Schacht, Unwin's, Brighton Borough Council

Cover photograph supplied by Floraprint

Printed in Italy

Contents

1 Floral display

For many home gardeners the highest achievement is a garden full of flowers – a riot of floral colour from spring to early autumn, to which herbaceous borders, rockeries, trees, and shrubs contribute. Annuals and other plants, assisted by spring bulbs, raised and planted out twice a year in beds and borders, will produce the most colourful displays. There is, however, a vast difference between a tasteful picture

A riotous mixture of colourful summer-blooming flowers for the herbaceous border here dazzlingly combines with flowering rock plants.

and the mere jumble of vivid floral colour that random planting will produce.

Enthusiasm for shapes, colours and scents is not enough in itself. The importance of plant form, and of the form, colour and texture of foliage should not be overlooked. These aspects can help to modulate the sheer brilliance of the blooms, and make possible tasteful arrays in which the different types of flower will complement

Far Left: A more modest mixture of flowering plants can be equally pleasing if planned with care.

A cheerful bed of attractively arranged spring flowers puts an end to winter's gloom and heralds warm days ahead.

Bedding plants graded in size and in contrasting colours relieve an otherwise austere design.

each other rather than set up in competition.

This can only be achieved by choosing good, healthy plants, creating for them the right setting in beds and borders which harmonise with the rest of the garden, and caring for them properly.

It is hoped that this book will help all gardeners to practise this popular form of gardening with understanding and inspiration. Better, more subtle effects can result from the same amount of effort and outlay (sometimes even less), yet will provide infinitely greater satisfaction. Working in this way, and knowing exactly what effects can be achieved, the gardener will be rewarded in ample measure by the results which ensue.

2 Making and preparing beds and borders

Sensible beds and borders in proportion to the surrounds and other features of the garden are the first essential. A few large beds are better than numerous small ones. They allow a greater range of plants to be grown without producing either a very flat or a top heavy picture and usually a much better effect is obtained, often with fewer plants. After-care is generally easier, too.

Avoid making beds of intricate shapes

like those shown here. They add to the difficulties of preparing, planting, edging round, and mowing between, and produce no better effect than beds of simple outline.

Also, avoid narrow ribbon borders of 60 cm (24 in) wide or less skirting a path or lawn or in front of the house. However planted, they will only emphasise straight lines; if a few plants make poor growth, the borders will look as if they are full of gaps, and they will also tend to dry out very quickly in times of drought.

When one display is over the old plants should be removed as quickly as possible and the beds dug over one spit deep. Well-rotted farmyard or mushroom-bed manure or compost can be incorporated at the same time, in the autumn for heavy and medium soils, in the spring for light, open soils.

Before raking down to produce a fine, level surface for planting, the soil must be made firm by treading. Use your heels rather than the balls of your feet for the greatest, most even pressure.

Beds and borders should be finished slightly higher than the surrounding ground but should never be mounded up. The finished level after treading and raking should be concave, sloping down gradually to just below the level of the turf or path. It should never be left like a plateau with steeply sloping sides, otherwise the soil round the edges may erode and the outer plants will suffer accordingly.

Intricate shaped beds make for hard labour and do not necessarily add to a garden's beauty. Simple designs are usually best.

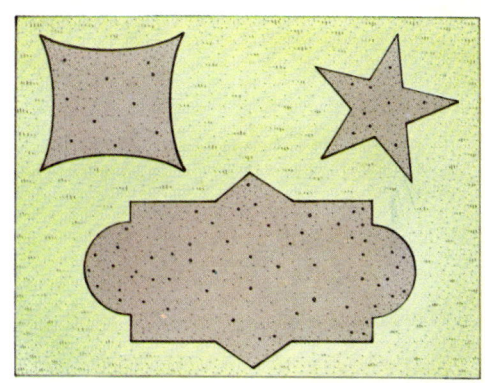

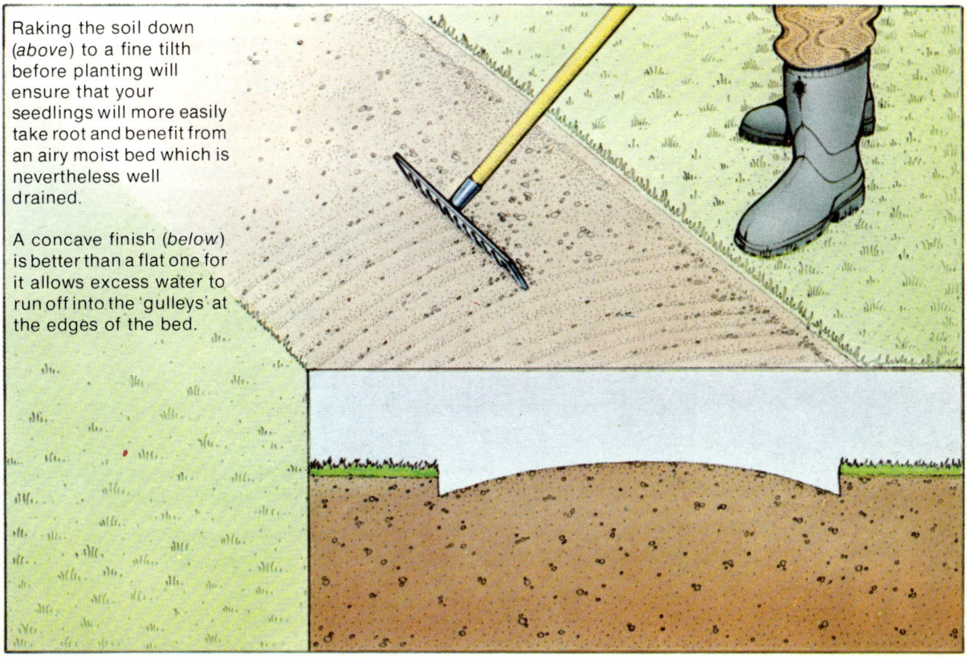

Raking the soil down (*above*) to a fine tilth before planting will ensure that your seedlings will more easily take root and benefit from an airy moist bed which is nevertheless well drained.

A concave finish (*below*) is better than a flat one for it allows excess water to run off into the 'gulleys' at the edges of the bed.

3 Raising your own plants

A small greenhouse is valuable but not vital.

A cold frame is needed to harden off the plants.

Glass on flat or edge-side-up bricks makes a useful temporary frame.

Cuttings can be rooted and seedlings can be raised on a window sill.

Anyone can raise at least some of the plants they require and thereby save some expense and often disappointment, of purchased plants.

With the aid of a small greenhouse, even an unheated one, or a lean-to conservatory attached to the house, one can raise a wide selection of plants, provided these temporary occupants are not deprived of light by the other, more permanent plants.

A cold frame is essential for hardening off plants. Even a knock-up frame constructed of boards nailed together or loose bricks with a polythene-covered light can be invaluable. Frames should be placed in a sunny position.

Cuttings of bedding geraniums, fuchsias, and other plants can be rooted in a small propagating case and grown on a window-sill. Marigolds, asters, alyssum and other plants which do not need to be sown until March can be raised in boxes. Turn them round each day to achieve balanced growth, eventually transferring them to the cold frame to harden off.

Suitable pans, pots and boxes will be required to accommodate plants, and compost in which to grow them. John Innes seed and potting composts can be bought ready mixed or you can use a soilless compost, i.e. peat with nutrients added.

Put roughage from the compost over the bottom of each receptacle to assist drainage, and fill to the rim with compost.

Press down lightly with the fingertips and level off.

Lightly firm to just below the rim with a levelling board or an empty pot.

Stand receptacles in water before sowing and allow to drain off. Sift a little fine compost over the surface if fine seeds are being sown. Scatter seeds very thinly over the surface. Large pelleted seeds may be spaced out separately.

Sift sufficient fine soil over the seeds to just cover them, and lightly press down. Leave very fine seeds uncovered. Cover with glass or polythene, and shade until seeds germinate.

Seedlings must be given plenty of light as soon as they germinate.

Prick out about 6 cm (2½ in) each way in other boxes as soon as large enough to handle. Lightly firm each seedling with forefinger and dibber.

Handle by the seed leaves, never the stem, which is easily damaged.

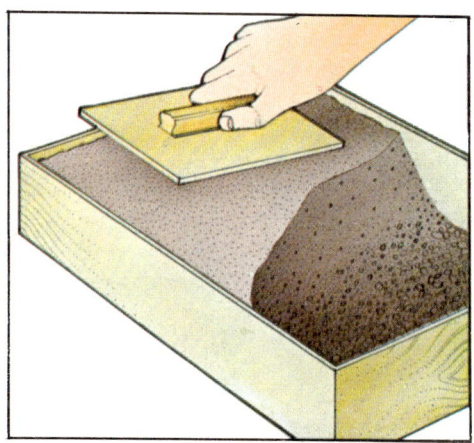

Left: First layer the bottom of the seed box with coarse material from the compost heap, then fill it to the brim with compost. Tamp down and smooth off.

Below left: Sow the seeds thinly in rows over the fine surface of the compost. Space pelleted seeds further apart. Cover both with a fine layer of soil.

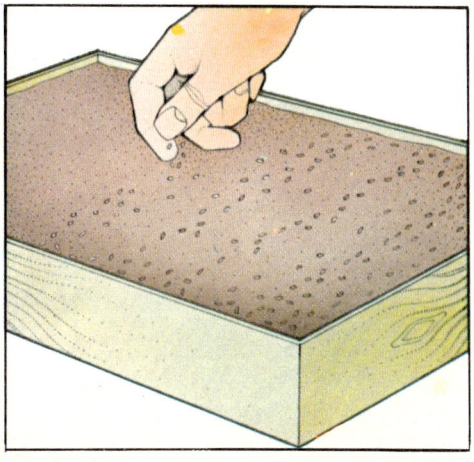

Above: To prick out seedlings successfully, pick them up carefully by the leaves to avoid damaging the delicate stems, insert the roots gently into holes prepared at regular intervals and press them gently in with the fingertips.

Above: Trim off the bottom leaves of the cutting and cut to a suitable length immediately below a node.

Above: Dahlia cuttings are best taken with the heel of the old stem.

Below: Insert the cuttings a reasonable distance apart in pots of peat and sand compost.

Below: When the cuttings have rooted, pot them individually into separate pots.

Lightly tap box to level the surface. Water in and keep as close to the light as possible. Take cuttings of such plants as fuchsias, zonal and ivy-leaved pelargoniums, *Iresine* and *Helichrysum rupestre* from plants in the beds at the end of August. Use a compost of 2 parts peat and 1 part sharp sand, and root under a propagating case in a greenhouse or on a shady windowsill. The pelargoniums do not need a propagating case and should be given very little water until rooted. Give the young plants full light and the minimum of heat during the winter. Pot off separately into small pots after the turn of the year using John Innes potting or a suitable soil-less compost. Pinch if necessary to obtain bushy plants and harden off by transferring to a cold frame in spring.

To obtain dahlia cuttings, cover old tubers with peat or soil, water and give heat to start them into growth in spring. Take the cuttings with a heel of the old stem and root in a shaded propagating case.

Wallflower (*Cheiranthus*) and *Myosotis* seed can be sown outside in shallow drills, about 25 cm (10 in) apart, in a prepared seed-bed in late May and June. Pansies, double daisies, aubrieta and Brompton stocks are best sown in boxes at about the same time and germinated in a cold frame. Polyanthus, primroses and *Primula denticulata* should be sown in April and also need a cold frame for germination, pricking off into boxes and hardening off as for summer bedding plants.

As soon as they are large enough, plant out the young plants for the summer 25–30 cm (10–12 in) apart, in rows about 30 cm (12 in) apart on any spare piece of ground or corner where they will get full sun. Polyanthus and primulas, however, should be planted in a more shaded position. Water in well and keep free from weeds. Daisies, pansies and aubrieta may be spaced out and grown on in deep boxes if spare ground is not available.

Later, lift them out carefully and plant in the beds and borders in the autumn when the summer bedding plants have finished flowering.

Polyanthus, primroses and *Primula*

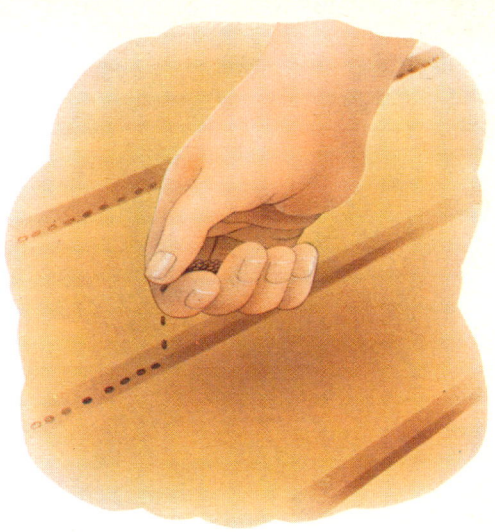

Sow spring bedding plants in shallow drills in the open.

denticulata may be grown on from year to year. When they have finished flowering, lift carefully with a fork, remove all old flowering stems and gently pull them apart into single crowns, each with some root attached. Plant out as many of the best crowns as required on a shady piece of ground for the summer, and make sure they do not lack water.

After flowering, propagate polyanthus and primroses by dividing the roots.

11

4 Purchasing plants

Choose your plants for bedding out with care. Choose healthy, robust plants which grow together thickly. Avoid spindly plants (left) selecting instead well-grown plants (right).

It is not usually safe to plant out summer bedding plants before the third week in May, later in cold districts. Plants are often on sale at garden centres and shops long before this – do not be tempted to buy even if your beds are ready to receive them.

Plants kept in boxes until sold are often weak and spindly by the time they are really ready to be planted out. It is then difficult to separate them without serious damage to the roots. Neither they nor pot-bound plants make rapid root growth when planted out and so suffer more from the move, especially if the weather is hot and dry. Spindly plants also tend to flop about and may not regain their natural bushy habit; likewise plants already well in flower, except, perhaps, *Alyssum*, *Tagetes* and French marigolds, which habitually start to flower when quite small. If it is possible to remove some of the flowers without spoiling the plants, this will be helpful.

In the autumn choose dwarf, bushy, sturdy plants, of wallflowers especially rather than large, lush ones which take longer to recover from the move and may not come through the winter so well.

5 Planting

The outer row excepted, slightly irregular staggered spacing is better than precise planting on the square system in straight rows or concentric circles. It is easier and quicker, and bare soil is not so obvious if the plants, for some reason or other, do not make their full growth.

Distances apart should be about 20–25 cm (8–10 in) each way for the dwarf edging plants; 30–35 cm (12–14 in) for salvias, petunias, intermediate antirrhinums, wallflowers and others of medium stature; 40–45 cm (16–18 in) for African marigolds, bedding geraniums, penstemons, annual rudbeckias and the taller zinnias; and 60 cm (24 in) or more for bedding dahlias. Tulips and narcissus bulbs which are to grow up through wallflowers, etc., need be no closer than 35 cm (14 in) each way.

If the ground is dry, water thoroughly some hours before planting. Plant at the correct depth, being careful not to plant too shallow. Firm well by hand and/or the handle of the trowel, and level out the soil between plants as you go.

Water in thoroughly, preferably individually, using an extension spout to the watering-can or an improvised lance to the hosepipe, to avoid treading on the beds. Water again as necessary until the plants are established. If the whole of the bed is watered, as the surface starts to dry, stir lightly to halt evaporation.

Above: Irregularly staggered spacing of the plants gives better coverage of the beds and promotes a fuller effect.

Below: An extension to the spout of the watering-can saves treading on the beds.

6 After-care

Careful hoeing on a dry day between the plants until they close up will keep down seedling weeds. When the plants meet they should effectively stifle most weeds; any weeds which do survive should be pulled out by hand.

Specimen or accent plants such as standard fuchsias and geraniums may need supporting, as inconspicuously as possible, with single stakes and ties, especially if the situation is exposed.

The ground-covering plants seldom need any support, but if for some reason they start to flop about and become untidy they are best held up by inserting a few bushy

Hoe on a sunny day to keep down weeds.

Support specimen plants with single stakes.

twigs which do not protrude above the plants.

Where practical, dead flowers or flowering heads are best removed as soon as they fade, for tidiness' sake and to prevent seeding and encourage continued flowering. This is very important in the case of antirrhinums, pansies, scarlet salvias, stocks and dahlias, where seed heads are conspicuous and soon affect flowering. It is not practical or necessary with *Alyssum, Lobelia, Impatiens,* begonias and others with numerous small flowers. Marigolds, petunias and verbenas usually continue to flower without any such aid, while asters and nemesias

tend to expend themselves in one long flush of bloom.

Spring bedding plants do not warrant this attention, as theirs is a comparatively short display with no follow on. It pays, however, to snap off the flowers of tulips just below the head either before or when they are lifted from the beds, so that the

Remove dead flowers for continuous blooming.

formation of seed pods does not hinder the building up of the bulbs for another year.

Insect pests are not usually much trouble. Greenfly is an occasional problem and is best controlled by spraying with a systemic insecticide. Sometimes the greenhouse whitefly is brought out on geraniums and fuchsias and continues to breed in a hot, dry summer. Malathion gives a better control than a systemic insecticide. Some plants are damaged by these substances, so read the directions carefully. Earwigs can be troublesome, especially on dahlias. Spraying against the other pests may help to keep them at bay, or they can be trapped in pots with a little dry moss laid inside among the plants. Inspect daily, destroying any catches.

White fly

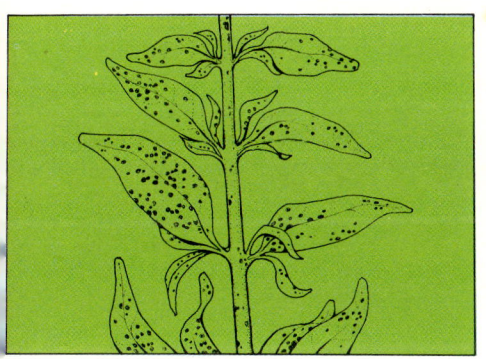

Antirrhinum rust

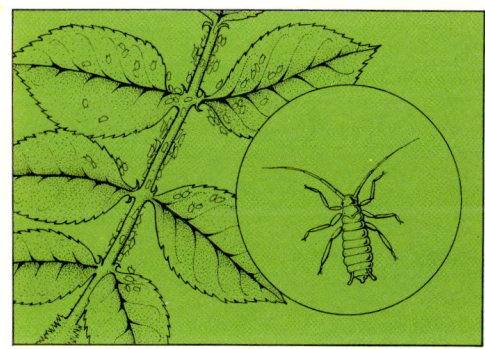

Aphis

Diseases are not much of a problem and one does not generally have to take any active steps to keep them in check. However, in southern areas of Britain, the brown fruiting bodies of antirrhinum rust on stems and leaves can be very crippling. This can be countered by planting modern rust-resistant varieties such as those in the Regal and Monarch strains. Wilt of China asters can mean the complete loss of plants. The stem blackens and shrivels just above ground level or a little higher, and the whole plant wilts and dies. Where it tends to be prevalent, it can also be countered by growing only resistant strains and varieties.

Earwig

7 Sowing hardy annuals in situ

If you do not wish to raise or purchase plants to bed out in the usual way, you can still have a lasting display of summer flowers by sowing seeds of hardy annuals where they are to flower. However, this means foregoing an April and May show of spring-flowering plants and bulbs. Dig the ground in the usual way, firm and rake down to a fine tilth, and then mark out irregularly shaped patches to a preconceived plan, with the tallest kinds in the centre – or at the back if the bed or border has one face only.

If necessary, thoroughly water the soil some hours before to ensure it is moist for sowing. Sow the seeds thinly from the end of March to early May. Either broadcast the seeds carefully over the surface and very lightly rake in; or sow in very shallow drills (little more than depressions in the soil) 25–40 cm (10–16 in) apart, according to the dimensions of each kind, carefully covering

To identify the flowers in the stylised border, see the diagram on the right and the key below: 1. *Clarkia* 'Salmon Queen' 2. *Linum grandiflorum* 3. *Phacelia campanularia* 4. *Chrysanthemum* tricolour 5. *Gypsophilia elegans* 'Pink' 6. *Godetia* (mixed) 7. Cornflower 'Blue Diadem' 8. Candytuft (mixed) 9. *Calendula* 'Orange Cockade' 10. *Nemophila insignis* 11. *Nigella* 'Miss Jekyll' 12. *Layia elegans* 13. *Eschscholzia* 'Ballerina' 14. Shirley poppy 15. *Chrysanthemum* 'Golden Gem'

each drill with fine soil when complete. Germination is often better by this latter method if a dry spell follows.

Weed seedlings usually germinate before the plants; remove them carefully by hand when quite small. Thin the plants in two stages – the first, when about 2–3 cm (¾–1¼ in) high, to half the final spacing, according to each kind's ultimate size. At the second and final thinning some unwanted plants can, if necessary, be carefully lifted and used to fill any large gaps.

After-care consists of little more than hand weeding until the plants can take care of themselves, and supporting with bushy twigs if necessary. Sometimes these twigs can be confined to the perimeter of a group of plants merely to prevent them flopping over their neighbours. With some dead-heading will help to prolong the display.

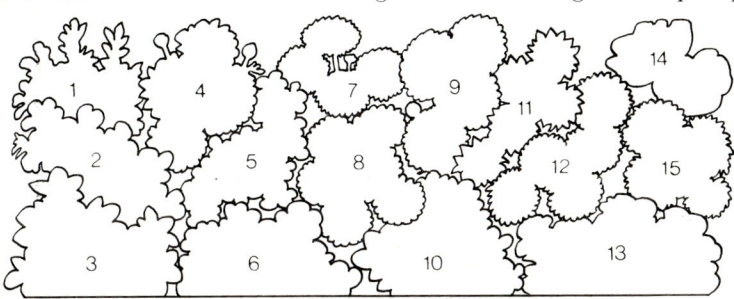

8 *Window boxes, plant containers and hanging baskets*

Even if you have only a backyard, or not even that, you can still enjoy the floral beauty of bedding plants by growing them in a variety of containers. If you have a garden, you may also like to decorate the house with window boxes and hanging baskets and have a few containers of plants on the terrace or patio.

Above: A summer window box will brighten the barest window and is ideal for city flat dwellers.

Today, these receptacles are available in many materials, shapes and designs – from simple, painted half-barrels and wooden window boxes to rectangular or round tubs, bowls, urns, vases, troughs, and more intricate shapes in asbestos, cement, stone, fibreglass, fibreglass-reinforced concrete, concrete or some form of plastic. Hanging baskets are now made in plastic as well as the traditional wire mesh, some with a built-in water reservoir, which helps to solve one of the main problems with this form of receptacle. Some are simple in design, some more ornate, including reproductions of Florentine, Regency, Victorian and other styles of the past.

Window boxes and containers must have adequate drainage holes, kept clear by covering with a layer of broken plant pots,

bricks, stones or other hardcore. In turn this must be covered with a layer of rough peat, half-rotted leaves or other coarse material to prevent the compost clogging up the drainage material.

A good, balanced, fairly rough compost is essential. John Innes No. 3 compost is suitable; if a little too fine it can be opened

Top: Brick pillars make attractive stands for plants.

Above: Group spring bulbs in containers.

up by the addition of coarse peat, which will also help to hold moisture. A suitable rough soilless compost can be used instead, but ordinary garden soil is generally unsuitable. When filling leave sufficient space, about 2·5–5 cm (1–2 in), after firming for watering purposes. It is advisable to replace the compost every two or three years as it tends to deteriorate both physically and nutritionally.

Wire hanging baskets need to be lined with sphagnum moss or plastic, perforated here and there to permit surplus water to drain away. All hanging baskets will need

Above: Hanging plants look decorative in doorways but must hang high enough not to block them.

Left: Standard fuchsias in tubs make splendid specimen plants to decorate doorway or patio.

new soil each time that they are planted.

After-care consists of diligent watering, never allowing the receptacles to get really dry; supporting specimen plants in an inconspicuous manner; feeding periodically with liquid manure or a complete fertiliser, applied always to moist soil; and removing flowers as soon as they fade to keep the display going.

Many of the summer bedding plants lend themselves to this form of culture. Bedding geraniums, fuchsias, begonias, *Impatiens*, heliotrope, marigolds, salvias and petunias are especially favoured. Dahlias, antirrhinums, nemesias, pansies and some of the hardy annuals are less suitable. Ivy-leaved pelargoniums, trailing lobelia and *Mesembryanthemum criniflorum* and others of a low,

19

spreading nature are invaluable for draping the sides of the containers. Climbing plants of annual duration can be successfully grown in containers for clambering up supports on the house walls. Many permanent plants can be grown in large containers, on their own or associated with bedding plants.

In the spring hyacinths, daffodils, narcissi and the various tulips can be grown along with the usual bedding plants such as wallflowers, forget-me-nots and polyanthus. Crocus, miniature daffodils, blue squills, dwarf iris and a host of other miniature bulbous subjects are very useful for window boxes. Aubrieta and *Arabis* are especially useful for draping over the sides.

Shade from buildings can be a problem, as most of the popular summer bedding plants do like plenty of sun. *Impatiens* and begonias are the best summer subjects for a partially shaded position, and most of the bulbs and spring-flowering plants, especially polyanthus, do reasonably well. Where the shade is absolute, it may be necessary to forgo bedding plants and turn to permanent, shade-loving subjects.

Complete your garden design and bring the garden into your house with a window box containing the same varieties as your herbaceous border.

9 *Selecting plants*

Summary bedding plants from cuttings

Note Throughout the following pages botanical names are shown in italics, In some cases, for simplicity, only popular names are given.

As most of the half-hardy plants propagated annually by vegetative means require a start in a greenhouse, less emphasis will be placed on plants grown from cuttings than on those plants readily raised from seed. Some in limited number can be raised on windowsills and in lean-to conservatories (see page 8) including the popular zonal pelargonium or bedding geranium and its forms, grown mainly for their coloured foliage.

In most cases cuttings have to be rooted in late summer and over-wintered under glass. A few quick-growing subjects such as *Iresine* can be left until spring. Bedding dahlias can be raised as described on page 10 but, as will be seen later, they are now very easily raised from seeds annually.

The hardy blue fescue grass (*Festuca glauca*) makes an excellent edging and foil for geraniums and other brightly-coloured flowers. Stock plants can be lifted in autumn, divided and, for convenience's

(*Pelargonium zonale*)

Festuca glauca

sake, wintered in a cold frame. Other accent foliage plants such as *Abutilon striatum* 'Thompsonii', with golden variegated leaves, and the silver-leaved *Helichrysum rupestre* and *H. microphyllum* are easily raised from late summer cuttings and none are more simple to root or quicker to develop than *Iresine lindenii*, with deep crimson foliage, and *I. herbstii* 'Aureo Reticulata', whose leaves are green splashed with gold with reddish veins.

plants in the beds or as specimens in large tubs. Varieties with a natural pendant habit are most graceful when trained as pyramids or standards.

Ordinary bushy plants of many of the indoor varieties of fuchsia are splendid for window boxes and containers, for which purpose it is best to raise them annually from late summer cuttings. Compact growing, free flowering varieties should be chosen. The single-flowered are often more adaptable than the large doubles. Many other plants which can spend summer in the beds can be grown by those with greenhouses and some means of providing heat

Pelargonium, ivy-leaved

The ivy-leaved pelargoniums are good value for those with the means for propagation and over-wintering. In beds they can be well spaced out as their trailing growths will cover quite a large area. This makes them excellent for hanging baskets and for draping over window boxes and other containers.

Those with a greenhouse can train up their own standard geraniums, fuchsias, *Helichrysum rupestre* and *Lantana*. This may take a couple of years, but by lifting before frost damages them, potting up and wintering in a cool greenhouse, and cutting back and shaping just prior to growth starting in the spring, they will last for several years.

Fuchsias in window box

Pelargonium crispum 'Variegatum', with small silvery, lemon-scented leaves, can be easily trained into close pyramidal form. Many fuchsias also make ideal pyramids, in which form they can be used as accent

when necessary. For the majority of home gardeners, however, plants which can easily and cheaply be raised from seed will be more practical and economical, and these are covered much more fully in the following pages.

Summer bedding plants from seed

Throughout the succeeding pages the following abbreviations are used: H.A., hardy annuals; H.H.A., half-hardy annuals; H.B., hardy biennials; H.P., hardy perennials; H.H.P., half-hardy perennials. An asterisk denotes hardy annuals, which can also be sown where they are to flower.

Ageratum. H.H.A. 12–25 cm (5–10 in). First-class edging plant. Fluffy flowers mainly in shades of powder-blue, some with mauve cast. Also white variety. Sow February/March in heat.

Alyssum maritimum. Sweet alyssum. H.A. 8–12 cm (3–5 in). The white varieties are the most popular but there are also lilac, purple and rose-pink forms. Sow in March and April.

Amaranthus. H.H.A. 60–90 cm (24–36 in). Varieties such as 'Molten Fire' and 'Illumination' make spectacular accent foliage plants. Sow in February/March in heat.

Anchusa capensis. H.A.* 20–25 cm (8–10 in). Dwarf and compact. The variety 'Blue Bird' is an intense shade of true blue. Good for window boxes. Sow in March.

Amaranthus 'Molten Fire'

Alyssum maritimum

Anchusa capensis 'Blue Bird'

Antirrhinum. Snapdragon.
H.P. The old and still popular intermediate kinds ran-
ging in height from 30 cm
(12 in) to 45 cm (18 in) have
been joined by such modern
strains as the rust-resistant
Monarch and Regal series.
Entirely new types include
the Coronette hybrids, with
the first central spike
surrounded by a cluster of
laterals, the hyacinth-
flowered, with pyramidal
spikes, and varieties with
open, penstemon-like flowers
lacking the usual pouch.

The new Pixies, with open
flowers on plants a mere
25 cm (10 in) high, are an
attractive addition to the
very dwarf Nanum Compac-
tion and Carpet types.

Antirrhinum 'Floral Carpet'

Taller varieties around
60–75 cm (24–30 in) in
height include the original
penstemon-flowered 'Bright
Butterflies' and 'Madame
Butterfly' (a variation with
double, azalea-like flowers),
base-branching varieties
and others going up to 90 cm
(36 in) in height.

Sow in January and
February in heat.

Antirrhinum 'Madame Butterfly'

Antirrhinum, penstemon-flowered

24

Aster. H.H.A. Bedding or China aster belonging to the genus *Callistephus* and not to *Aster* proper which includes the popular Michaelmas daisies. There is a wide range of types and heights, including disease-resistant strains. All make an excellent display in beds from midsummer onwards.

The flowers of the taller strains, 45–75 cm (18–30 in) high, vary in form from the neat rounded blooms of the Ball or Bouquet strains to the large shaggy flowers of the old Ostrich Plumes. Most, especially the single-flowered varieties, make excellent long-lasting cut flowers.

The dwarf asters are ideal for formal beds. Modern strains such as Milady have large double flowers on bushy plants no more than 30 cm (12 in) high and as much across. Pinocchio is even more dwarf and has neat little flowers. Then there are the somewhat taller, pompon-flowered Lilliputs, the semi-double Pepite strain and others.

All the foregoing are available in well-varied mixtures, some of them in separate colour varieties. Sow in March and early April.

Aster 'Powderpuffs' (Bouquet type)

Aster, dwarf bedding type

Begonia semperflorens.
Fibrous-rooted begonia.
H.H.P. 15–25 cm (6–10 in).
Many modern strains and
cultivars are now available,
either in mixture or individual varieties in colours
from white through shades of
pink to deep scarlet, some
with deep purple/maroon
foliage. Continuous-
flowering but not always
successful in colder districts.
Sun or partial shade. Sow
December/January
in heat.

Begonia, intermediate bedding. 20–30 cm (8–12 in).
Hybrids such as the Danica
series, which make rather
larger plants than *B.
semperflorens*, have a good
range of colours, some with
shiny bronze foliage.

Begonia semperflorens

Begonia, intermediate bedding

Strains of tuberous begonias
and others, ideal for hanging
baskets and window boxes,
can now be raised from seed
to flower the same season.
They require sowing in
December/January, so a
heated greenhouse is really a
necessity.

Cineraria maritima

Cleome spinosa

Coleus

Coleus. Flame nettle. 30–40 cm (12–16 in). Dwarf strains of these greenhouse foliage plants are now available from seed and used to supplement flowers in summer beds of more favoured districts. Sow in heat in February.

Cleome spinosa. Spider flower. H.H.A. 90–100 cm (36–40 in). Unusual flowering plants for the centres of large beds, for use as accent plants or for large containers. They flower throughout the summer. Purple, rose and white forms Sow February/March in hea

Cineraria maritima. H.H.P. 15–30 cm (6–12 in). Not to be confused with the popular greenhouse annuals. Several different varieties, all with elegant silver foliage, which are very useful for accent plants and for toning down bright floral colours. Sow in February in heat.

Convolvulus 'Tricolour'

Convolvulus. H.A. 20–30 cm (8–12 in). Forms of *C. minor* are non-climbing plants allied to the bellbine. Trumpet-shaped flowers in a mixture of colours. Deep blue variety with white throat also available. Good for tubs and window boxes. Sow in February in heat.

Dahlia. **H.H.P.** 30 cm (12 in) plus. Bedding dahlias of various heights with flowers of most of the popular types, i.e. single, double, cactus, collarette, pompone, etc., can now be so easily raised from seeds annually that it is not worth while storing the tubers and raising plants from cuttings each season. Sow in February in heat.

Dianthus. Pink. 15–30 cm (6–12 in). Modern bedding strains derived from perennial species are grown as **H.H.A.**, flower early and freely and produce brilliant displays in mixture or as separate varieties. Sow February/March and grow cool.

Echium. **H.A.*** Bugloss. 30 cm (12 in). Open flowers on bushy plants in a mixture of soft tones of pink, blue, lilac, purple and white. Blue available as a separate variety. Sow in March and in April.

Dahlia, Coltness hybrids

Dahlia, Unwin's hybrids

Dianthus sinensis 'Magic Charms'

Gazania splendens 'Grandiflora'

Echium, dwarf hybrids

Euphorbia marginata. Snow-on-the-mountain. H.A.* 60 cm (24 in). Soft green leaves variegated with silver. Inconspicuous flowers surrounded by white bracts. Good accent plant. Sow in March.

Gazania. H.H.P. 24–30 cm (10–12 in) South African daisies in brilliant mixtures of yellow, orange, pink, red and bronze shades, many attractively zoned. They revel in full sun. Good for window boxes and tubs. Sow in February in heat.

Euphorbia marginata

Geranium 'Sprinter'

Impatiens, mixed

Geranium. Zonal pelargonium. H.H.P. 45 cm (18 in). Now possible to raise these popular bedding plants from seed. New dwarf early-flowering varieties such as 'Chérie', 'Sprinter' and 'Ringo' are now taking the place of the original varieties and are very freeflowering. Sow in heat January/February.

Heliotrope. Cherry pie. H.H.P. 40–45 cm (16–18 in). Lavender to deep purple flowers, some varieties with purplish foliage. Highly valued for its sweet scent. Good for window boxes and containers. Sow in February in heat.

Impatiens. Busy lizzie. H.H.P. 10–25 cm (4–10 in). Dwarf, spreading and continuous-flowering. Does well in shade. Suitable for window boxes and containers. Sold as mixtures or separate varieties in white, orange, salmon, pink, rose and scarlet, some with striped flowers, some with bronze foliage. Sow in early March in heat.

Heliotrope 'Marine'

Lobelia 'Kaiser Wilhelm'

Lobelia. H.H.P. 10–15 cm (4–6 in). Along with sweet alyssum the most popular edging subject, especially the deep blue, Cambridge blue and blue/white eye varieties. Also available in white, red with white eye and a mixture of colours. The trailing forms are invaluable for draping hanging baskets, window boxes and other containers. Sow January/February in heat. Do not cover the seed when sowing and prick out in groups of 2–4 rather than individual seedlings.

Mesembryanthemum criniflorum. Livingstone daisy. H.H.A. 8–15 cm (3–6 in). Sprawling plants of a succulent nature specially suitable to a hot dry position, thus ideal for trailing over the edges of window boxes and containers in full sun. The type is rose pink but modern mixed strains include other brilliant colours. Sow February/March in heat.

Mesembryanthemum criniflorum

Lobelia 'Sapphire'

31

Marigold. H.H.A. The African or American marigolds have arisen from *Tagetes erecta* and are available in heights of 20–90 cm (8–36 in). Those of medium height are probably the most valuable for the home garden. All have large almost globular heads of flower varying from pale primrose through lemon and gold to deep orange.

The French marigolds are forms of *Tagetes patula* and are smaller in all their parts than the Africans. Heights vary from the 15 cm (6 in) dwarfs suitable for edging to those around 35 cm (14 in). Mahogany-red, in whole or in part, is the latest addition to the colour range and the flowers may be fully double, single or have a distinct central crest.

A new race of hybrids between the Africans and the French has been introduced recently. In habit and type of flower these hybrids more closely approach the French but the flowers are larger and the plants grow to 25–35 cm (10–14 in) high.

All these marigolds are quick to develop. To avoid them becoming tall and drawn before planting out they should not be sown earlier than late March or early April.

Marigold, African, 'Gold Coins'

Marigold, French, 'Naughty Marietta'

Matricaria. Feverfew. H.P. 20–25 cm (8–10 cm). Modern dwarf kinds may have ball-shaped flowers, or the boss of disc florets may be surrounded by a single row of flat florets. Very adaptable, they flower over a long period. Sow in March.

Nasturtium. H.A.* 20–30 cm (8–12 in). Non-climbing forms now available in a variety of bright colours. Good for poor dry soil and for hanging baskets and window boxes. Sow in March in small pots, one seed per pot.

Nemesia. H.H.A. 20–30 cm (8–12 in). Most popular as a mixture but can be had in separate colours of yellow, orange, scarlet, pink and blue, also bicolours. Early and profuse of flower. Sow in March.

Pansy and viola. H.P. 15–20 cm (6–8 in). Available in mixture or in separate colours. Violas generally have smaller flowers in a more limited colour range but stand heat and drought better. Sow from January to March.

Nemesia hybrids

Pansy, mixed giants

Nicotiana. Flowering tobacco. H.H.A. 25–90 cm. (10–36 in). Available in different heights with white or crimson flowers, also strains including pastel shades and an attractive lime green variety. Sow in February in heat.

Nicotiana affinis hybrids

33

Penstemon hybrids

Petunia Multiflora 'Pale Face'

Penstemon. Beard tongue. H.P. 45–75 cm (18–30 in). Sold as a mixture in mainly pink, red and purplish shades, some with white or striped throats. Long season of flowering and good for cutting. Sow January/February in heat.

Petunia. Multiflora type. H.H.A. 25–30 cm (10–12 in). These have smaller flowers and are rather more profuse of bloom than the Grandifloras on page 35. Also they are rather less susceptible to bad weather so more reliable for bedding purposes. Good weather-resistant strains have been developed. Can be had in a wide range of brilliant colours, including striped and chequered varieties. Sow January to March in heat.

Petunia Multiflora 'Starfire'

Petunia Grandiflora

Petunia Multiflora Double

Petunia. Grandiflora type. H.H.A.
25–35 cm (10–14 in). These have larger
flowers than the Multifloras, some with
waved petals, and are available as
individual varieties in a range of brilliant
colours – self, chequered or bicolour.
They are better for window-box and tub
culture than for planting in the beds, but
weather-resistant strains are being
developed. Sow January to March in heat.
Petunia. Double-flowered type. H.H.A.
30–35 cm (12–14 in). Both the Multifloras
and Grandifloras have double-flowered
strains with large, ruffled flowers up to
10 cm (4 in) across in a wide range of self-
and bicolors. Some strains are sweetly
scented. Generally used for pot culture but
also suitable for window boxes and tubs in
the more favoured districts, if not for
display in the beds. Sow from January to
March in heat.
Phlox drummondii. H.H.A. 15–30 cm
(6–12 in). Both tall and dwarf strains are
available as individual varieties or
mixtures in a wide range of colours
including blue and violet. The dwarf
strains are good for window boxes. Sow
February/March in heat.

Phlox drummondii, Beauty strain

Ricinus zanzibarensis

Portulaca. Sun plant. H.H.A. 15 cm (6 in).
Dwarf and spreading with fleshy leaves.
Likes a hot, dry, sunny position so is very
suitable for filling in on the rockery and for
tubs and window boxes. Generally sold as a
mixture of brilliant shades of rose, orange,
scarlet, crimson, rosy purple, yellow and
white, many with double flowers. Sow
February/March in heat.

Ricinus. Castor-oil plant. H.H.A. Will reach
130 cm (52 in) or more when planted out. A
splendid accent plant with large shiny
leaves but suitable only for limited use in
large beds or as a tall architectural plant in
a tub. *R. gibsonii* has deep bronze leaves and
stems while *R. zanzibarensis* has green leaves
with prominent mid-ribs. Sow singly in
small pots January/February in heat.

Rudbeckia. Cone flower. H.H.A. 40–90 cm
(16–36 in). Dwarf forms, such as the Rustic
Dwarfs with large flowers in rich yellow,
bronze and mahogany, and 'Marmalade'
(golden-yellow with black central cone),
make the best bedding plants. The Gloriosa
Daisy type are taller with larger flowers. All
are excellent for cut flowers. Sow in
February and grow cool.

Rudbeckia, annual form

Salpiglossis. H.H.A.
45–70 cm (18–28 in).
Delightful mixture of
colours, many flowers veined
and chequered with different
shades. Must have plenty of
sun, therefore suitable only
for more favoured areas. Sow
January–March in heat.
Stock. H.H.A. 25–60 cm
(10–24 in). Ten-week and
other summer-flowering
stocks vary mainly in height,
season of flower and size of
spike. With some strains it is
possible to obtain a higher
percentage of doubles by
discarding either the weaker
or the dark green seedlings.
Sow February–March.
Salvia splendens. H.H.A.
15–30 cm (6–12 in). Several
different scarlet varieties
varying only in height, time
of commencing to flower or
foliage. Purple, rose and
pink forms also available.
Sow January–March in heat.
Tagetes signata 'Pumila'
H.H.A. 15–20 cm (6–8 in).
Differs from French
marigolds in its finer foliage
and its very small flowers in
shades of lemon, yellow,
orange or red. A useful
edging plant. Sow in March.

Salvia splendens

Tagetes signata 'Pumila'

Salpiglossis

Verbena hybrida 'Nana Compacta'

Ursinia. H.H.A. 15–20 cm (6–8 in). *U. anethoides* is a South African daisy with orange flowers and reddish central zone. Other hybrid strains in lemon to orange tones. Requires a sunny position. Sow February/March in heat.

Venidium. Monarch of the Veldt. H.H.A. 60–90 cm (24–36 in). *V. fastuosum* is a South African daisy with orange flowers with black centres. Hybrid strains have white, cream, lemon and orange shades. Pleasing woolly foliage. Sow February/March in heat.

Verbena. Vervain H.H.A. 15–30 cm (6–12 in). Available in mixtures or separate colours including violet-blue; some have conspicuous white eyes. Useful for window boxes and tubs. Sow January/March in heat.

Venidium fastuosum

Zinnia, dahlia-flowered

Zinnia. H.H.A. Zinnias do best in warm, sunny summers. Weather- and disease-resistant strains are now being developed. The tallest varieties are suitable for large beds and cut flowers. They may have flat or quilled florets. The dwarfer kinds range from the Lilliputs, 30 cm (12 in), with ball-shaped flowers, the Persian Carpet type, 30 cm (12 in), with small double and semi-double flowers, many of them bicoloured, the compact Buttons strain 25–30 cm (10–12 in), the newer Peter Pan hybrids with large flowers on 25–30 cm (10–12 in) high plants down to the Thumbelina varieties with small double and semi-double flowers on 15 cm (6 in) plants. Some are available in separate colour varieties. Sow in March in heat.

Zinnia, Lilliput

Calliopsis

Calendula, hybrids

Hardy annuals for growing in situ

Amaranthus caudatus. Love-lies-bleeding. 60 cm (24 in). Long red drooping racemes of flower like lambs'-tails. A form with greenish-white flowers also available. Best on a soil that is not too rich. Thin to not less than 35 cm (14 in) for the best effect.
Calendula. Pot marigold. 30–60 cm (12–24 in). An old favourite now available with double, quilled centre and incurved flowers in lemon, yellow and orange selfs and mixtures of cream, apricot, flame and bicolors. Remove dead heads regularly for long flowering. Thin to 25–50 cm (10–20 in) apart.

Amàranthus caudatus

Candytuft. 25–35 cm
(10–14 in). One of the most
popular hardy annuals,
quick to come into flower.
Thrives in most soils and will
succeed in sun or partial
shade. Available in mixture
or separate colours of white,
red, pink, rose, lilac and
crimson-purple. Sweetly
scented. Thin to 25–30 cm
(10–12 in).

Chrysanthemum. 15–75 cm
(6–30 in). Several different
annual chrysanthemums
have excellent garden
strains. There are the dwarf
spreading *C. multicaule* with
yellow flowers, *C. carinatum*
(tricolour) varieties with
zoned flowers in bright
colours, the garden versions
of the corn marigold, *C.
segetum* and the double-
flowered *C. coronarium* in yellow and primrose. All have
finely cut elegant foliage and
are useful for cutting. Thin
to a distance slightly less
than their height.

Candytuft 'Mercury' ('Giant Tetra')

Chrysanthemum carinatum
(Tricolour)

Calliopsis. Annual coreopsis.
25–50 cm (10–20 in). The
taller varieties have mainly
golden-yellow and orange-
yellow flowers, some with a
maroon zone. The dwarf
forms also include dark red
shades, some with a gold
border. Thin dwarf forms to
25 cm (10 in), taller varieties
to 35–45 cm (14–18 in).

Cornflower. 30–90 cm (12–28 in). The dwarf – 30–40 cm (12–16 in) high – varieties are the most suitable, although the really tall ones can be used in a wide border and their flowers are very useful for cutting. Both can be had in mixture or in separate colours including white, shades of red, pink and rose, and true cornflower blue. Thin the dwarfs to 25–30 cm (10–12 in), the taller kinds to 40–50 cm (16–20 in), at which height they should support each other.

Clarkia elegans. 50–60 cm (20–24 in). Long, slender stems of double flowers on bushy plants which usually need a little support. Long season of bloom. Can be had in mixture or in distinct varieties with white, pink, rose, salmon, orange-scarlet, scarlet and purple flowers. Do not thin too closely: at 35–45 cm (14–18 in) apart, the plants should support each other without detriment to the display.

Cornflower (*Centaurea cyanus*)

Clarkia elegans

Dimorphotheca aurantiaca hybrids

Cynoglossum amabile 'Firmament'

Eschscholzia californica hybrids

Cynoglossum. Hound's tongue. 45–55 cm (18–22 in). Small true turquoise-blue flowers are freely produced, also a white form. Flowers throughout the summer and is not averse to partial shade. Thin to about 30 cm (12 in) apart.

Dimorphotheca. Star of the Veldt. 25–35 cm (10–14 in). Large daisy-like flowers in yellow, orange, salmon-orange shades and white. Comes into flower quickly and continues throughout the summer if dead blooms are removed. Thin to about 25 cm (10 in) apart.

Eschscholzia. Californian poppy. 15–30 cm (6–12 in). Free-flowering plants with finely cut foliage and single, semi-double or double flowers in a brilliant range of colours. Likes plenty of sun and is not particular as to soil. Thin to about 20 cm (8 in) apart.

Godetia. 20–60 cm (8–24 in). Long-flowering colourful annuals with single, semi-double or double flowers, many with frilled petals, in colours from white through pink and red shades to crimson plus lavender-blue, some composed of more than one colour. Some are available as separate varieties. Thin the dwarfer kinds to about 20 cm (8 in), the taller ones to 30–45 cm (12–18 in) apart.

Helianthus annuus. Sunflower. The common annual sunflower growing to a height of 2 m (6 ft) or more is obviously much too tall for the average annual border. There are now dwarf forms no more than 60 cm (24 in) high, some with single, and some with double flowers. They are good plant-makers, so thin them to about the same distance as their height.

Helianthus annuus 'Yellow Pygmy'

Gypsophila elegans. 45 cm (18 in). Graceful sprays of small white or pink flowers which are also useful for mixing with larger flowers in floral arrangements. Thin to about 35 cm (14 in) apart.

Lavatera. Mallow. 75–90 cm (30–36 in). Suitable for large borders. Needs little or no support. Large rose, pink or white trumpet-shaped flowers. Good plant-makers, they should be thinned to stand not less than 60 cm (24 in) apart.

Gypsophila elegans alba

Leptosiphon. Stardust. 10–15 cm (4–6 in). Finely cut foliage and masses of tiny star-like flowers in various shades. Very dwarf and ideal for the front of the border or for temporarily filling bare spots on a rockery. Thin to 15 cm (6 in) apart.

Larkspur. Annual delphinium. 75–120 cm (30–48 in). Invaluable for the character of its long spikes of white, pink, salmon, rose, scarlet, lilac and blue flowers. A dwarfer form has recently been introduced. Available as mixtures or separate colours. They can be thinned to distances much less than their height.

Larkspur, Giant Imperial mixed

Lavatera trimestris, mixed

Leptosiphon hybridus, mixed

Lupinus, Hartwegii strain

Linum. Flax. 30–40 cm (12–16 in). *L. grandi-florum* in crimson-scarlet or white with crimson centre is an excellent hardy annual. The slightly taller common blue flax is also well worth growing. Thin to 25–30 cm (10–12 in) apart.

Lupinus. 40–90 cm (16–36 in). The annual lupins can be had as a colourful mixture of tall kinds or as the dwarf Pixie strain and, like the perennial kinds, they are very showy border plants. Thin to 30–40 cm (12–16 in) apart.

Lonas inodora. 30–35 cm (12–14 in). A South African daisy with small, tightly packed heads of yellow flowers on branching stems with finely cut foliage. A useful secondary plant when grown as an H.H.A. and also good for drying for winter decorations. Thin to 30 cm (12 in) apart.

Linaria. Toadflax. 20–30 cm (8–12 in). Spikes of small snapdragon-like flowers in mixtures of pink to red, purple and yellow shades, including bicolours. Suitable for the front of the border and for cutting. Thin to 20 cm (8 in) apart.

Linaria 'Fairy Bouquet'

Nemophila insignis

Nemophila insignis. Baby Blue Eyes. 15 cm (6 in). Sweet little plant for the front of the border. Sky-blue flowers with white centres. Likes a hot, dry situation. Thin to 15–20 cm (6–8 in) apart.

Nigella. Love-in-a-mist. 40–45 cm (16–18 in). Cornflower-like flowers within a ring of fine leaves followed by attractive inflated seed pods, but better succession of blooms if these are removed. Blue and rose-pink varieties, also mixture of these colours with lavender, mauve and purple. Good for cutting. Thin to 35–40 cm (14–16 in) apart.

Mignonette (*Reseda odorata*). 30 cm (12 in). An old favourite valued more for its sweet fragrance than the form or colour of its spikes of reddish or yellowish flowers. Germinates best when the soil has been well firmed before sowing. Attracts bees. Thin to 25–30 cm (10–12 in) apart.

Nigella damascena 'Miss Jekyll'

Mignonette

Ornamental grasses. Groups of annual grasses with ornamental flowering plumes can add to the distinction of the annual border and provide valuable material for drying for winter decorations. They may be used in mixture, or preferably, in distinct kinds. One of the most popular is the quaking grass, *Briza maxima*, with nodding spikelets. The cloud grass, *Agrostis nebulosa*, has broad feathery panicles, the hare's-tail grass, *Lagurus ovatus*, oval white downy plumes and the squirrel-tail grass, *Hordeum jubatum*, 5 cm- (2 in-) long silky tassels with even longer barley-like awns.

Briza maxima
Hordeum jubatum

Poppy. 45–90 cm (18–36 in). The Shirley poppies with single, semi-double or fully double flowers, the carnation-flowered and the peony-flowered are all first-class, fairly tall, long-flowering annuals available in mixtures of bright warm colours. Thin to a little less than their height apart.

Poppy, Shirley mixed

Sweet william 'Indian Carpet'

Phacelia campanularia

Phacelia campanularia. 22 cm (9 in). Dwarf plant for the front of the rockery with true gentian-blue bell-shaped flowers beloved of bees. Thin to about 20 cm (8 in) apart.
Sweet william. 15 cm (6 in). Very dwarf forms of the popular early summer-flowering sweet william flower very quickly when grown as hardy annuals. Sold as a mixture in shades of pink and red with white. Thin to 15 cm (6 in).

Viscaria, mixed

Sweet sultan. 45–60 cm (18–24 in). Long-stemmed, sweetly-scented fringed blooms in a mixture of many colours. Good for cutting. Thin to a little less than their height.

Sweet scabious. 40–90 cm (16–36 in). Generally sold as a mixture of many colours from white to deep maroon. Thin to a little less than their height.

Viscaria. 20–40 cm (8–16 in) Single flax-like flowers in blue, pink, red and white in mixtures or separate colours Thin to a little less than their height.

Virginian stock. 22 cm (9 in). Useful little plant for the front of the border or the rockery. Small flowers in mixture of many colours. Thin slightly.

Sweet sultan

Morning glory (*Ipomaea*)

Annual climbing plants

Annual climbers are particularly useful for
tub culture on patios to grow up wires or
other supports on walls or fences.

Canary creeper (*Tropaeolum canariense*)

Canary creeper. H.A.
Fringed canary-yellow
flowers all summer. Grows
in sun or shade and is also
useful for draping window
boxes and tubs in addition to
covering fences or walls. Sow
in situ in April or early May
or, if more convenient, in
small pots for planting out
later. Sow one or two seeds in
each pot and later thin to one
plant.

Morning glory. H.H.A. A
lovely climber for a sunny
position, especially the variety 'Heavenly Blue'. White,
scarlet and blue-striped
white varieties also obtain-
able. The flowers last for a
morning only, hence the
name, but are produced in
succession for many weeks.
Soak seed in water for 24
hours before sowing in small
pots in heat in March as for
Canary creeper.

51

Nasturtium (*Tropaeolum majus*), Gleam hybrids

Nasturtium. H.A. The climbing forms have single or semi-double spurred flowers in a variety of colours. They are less rampant and more floriferous in dry rather poor soils. They do well as hanging plants in window boxes and containers. Sow in situ in April or early May or if more convenient in small pots as for canary creeper and plant out later.

Sweet pea. *Lathyrus odoratus*. H.A. Very popular with numerous varieties and colours. Usually grown primarily for cut flowers but also make splendid plants for summer covering of walls and fences growing in the open ground or in tubs. Flowers must be cut off as they fade to maintain a succession of blooms. Soak seeds in water for two days before sowing in small pots from January to March in heat, or in September and October and winter in a cold frame.

Sweet pea, mixed

Spring bedding plants from seed

Bellis perennis 'Monstrosa' white

Aubrieta. H.P. 10 cm (4 in). This popular rockery plant makes an excellent subject for the spring beds with its low cushions of mauve, purple, pink or carmine flowers, most colours available separately. Sow as advised on page 11 or lift after flowering, divide and plant out for the summer. *Bellis perennis.* Double-flowered daisies. H.P. 10–15 cm (4–6 in). The Monstrosa type has flowers up to 2·5 cm (1 in) across. The Pomponettes are dwarfer and have smaller pompon-like flowers with quilled florets. Pink, rose-red and white flowers in mixture or separately. Ideal for edging or under dwarf tulips. *Cheiranthus allionii.* Siberian wallflower. H.P. 30–40 cm (12–16 in). Slightly later flowering than the ordinary wallflower, extending its season into June. The type has rich orange flowers and there are golden and apricot versions.

Aubrieta, mixed

53

Myosotis. Forget-me-not. H.B. 15–40 cm (6–16 in). The only true blue spring bedding plant. Pink and white varieties are available but these do not have the same appeal. The taller varieties vary in the depth of tone of their flowers. The dwarf forms, including a good rose-coloured variety, make very compact plants ideal for edging or for small beds.

Pansy. Heart's-ease. H.P. 15–20 cm (6–8 in). Numerous strains and varieties are available as mixtures or separately in white, yellow, orange, apricot, rose, red, rich wine, blue, violet-blue and purple. Some are completely self-coloured, others have the typical dark purple

Pansy, winter-flowering type
Pansy, 'Clear Crystals' type

Myosotis, dwarf type

54

or purplish-black blotch in the centre. Winter and spring strains are used for spring bedding and are seldom without a few flowers during any mild spell in winter, coming into full flower in April and May.

Polyanthus. H.P. 20–30 cm (8–12 in). Most popular as a brilliant mixture in white, yellow, pink to rose, red to crimson and blue, many with yellow eyes. Some colours are available separately, of which blue is very valuable. Beware of the very large-flowered strains grown for pot work; they are generally less profuse of bloom and do not always stand cold weather well.

Polyanthus, mixed

Primrose. H.P. 15 cm (6 in).
Differs from the polyanthus
in that the flowers are
produced singly instead of in
heads. Generally a little earlier to flower. Now available
in much the same range of
colour. Choose only the fully
hardy strains for bedding.

Primrose, modern strain

Primula denticulata. Drum-
stick primula. H.P.
30–40 cm (12–16 in). Not
used for spring bedding as
much as it might be. Can be
raised and treated in the
same way as polyanthus.
The type has medium mauve
flowers, but there are much
deeper-coloured versions,
also pink, red and white
forms, the latter the tallest of
all. Narcissi and the
earliest flowering tulips are
its best companions. Not
really suitable for container
cultivation.

Wallflower (*Cheiranthus
cheiri*). H.P. 20–45 cm
(8–18 in). Spring bedding is
incomplete without the
seductive scent of
wallflowers. The standard
kinds are available in white,
primrose, yellow, orange,
pink, scarlet, ruby, blood-
red and purple shades.
'Eastern Queen' is of a shade
in which apricot
predominates and there are
other pastel shades usually
incorporated in mixtures.
The dwarf or Tom Thumb
forms have many uses and
often stand the winter better
than the taller kinds in
exposed places, although
their range of colours is not
quite so extensive. They are
better than the taller kinds
for container cultivation.

Primula denticulata

Wallflowers, mixed

Spring bedding bulbs

Hyacinths. Probably best planted on their own in beds as they do not mix too readily with the usual spring bedding subjects. Ideal for colourful effects in window boxes and other receptacles. Choose bedding-type bulbs, i.e. those of second size, which are cheaper and produce rather smaller and more graceful flowering spikes.

Narcissus 'Sempre Avanti'

Narcissus 'Flower Record'

Narcissus. Includes the Trumpet daffodils although these are generally less suitable for formal bedding than the groups with smaller trumpets which are usually a little later to flower and are rather lighter in flower and foliage. The Tazetta or bunch-flowered and the double kinds are not really suitable.

Narcissi usually look best in a natural setting – in grass, or on a rockery, for example. They can, however, be used in the beds with early-flowering subjects such as *Primula denticulata* and primroses as groundwork. They are always acceptable for bringing an early breath of spring to window boxes and r receptacles.

Hyacinths, mixed

The bedding season begins with the large brilliant blooms of forms of *Tulipa fosteriana* and the early single tulips which can be used either on their own or grown with primroses or *Primula denticulata*. For the latter the taller varieties of the early singles, such as 'General de Wet', 'Dr Plesman' and 'Prince of Austria' should be chosen, all of which are sweetly scented.

Early single tulip 'Pink Beauty'

Early double tulips

The Triumph tulips flower second and being of medium height are fine for growing with polyanthus. The early double tulips flower about the same time. Being quite dwarf they are best used over a low groundwork of pansies, double daisies or dwarf forget-me-nots.

When individual beds and borders are devoted to seasonal bedding, the happy associations created in them should also blend in with other features in the garden. Although personal taste will naturally enter into colour blending, there are certain basic principles to follow. The colour extremes are the soft tones of blue, mauve and pink and the harder tones of white, orange, deep yellow, crimson and scarlet. A soft tone can be used to relieve the intensity of a hard one, e.g. pale pink with crimson or blue with deep yellow. Dark purples also require some relief. Magenta tones are difficult to associate with other colours.

Foliage is particularly useful as a foil for floral colour. Grey and silver especially will effectively break up and tone down bright and the less sociable colours. Golden and variegated foliage must be used with care: too much can produce effects which are either harsh or spotty. That of a deep crimson or purple tone has many uses but must not be overdone otherwise the picture will become sombre. The surrounds of adjacent permanent plants may decide whether a quiet harmonious combination or something rather more vivid is required. A dull situation will almost certainly call for a bright combination of colours.

Above: A bright association of scarlet salvias interplanted with *Coleus* 'Golden Ball', with the variegated *Abutilon savitzii* as an accent plant. The whole is surrounded by an edging of white *Alyssum*.
Left: A low and more subtle blend of the soft colours of pink fibrous-rooted begonias with white and violet *Alyssum* and dot plants of the silver-foliaged *Cineraria maritima*.

Although the range of subjects is much more limited spring bedding offers great scope for colour planning. It is difficult to avoid a two- or three-tier effect in the beds but this seldom becomes boring. The blue of forget-me-nots (*Myosotis*) is invaluable either as a main groundwork or in combination with any tone of wallflower. Use wallflowers on their own either in a single colour or in two harmonising tones mixed together. Fully mixed strains are seldom as pleasing as individual colours or planned combinations – either of wallflowers on their own or overplanted with tulips.

Polyanthus and primroses must be kept on their own, with tulips of suitable type as their sole companions – for they flower somewhat earlier than wallflowers, *Myosotis*, *Bellis* and pansies. The last two subjects, together with the dwarf compact forms of *Myosotis*, make ideal edgings for wallflower combinations, providing blue, purple and white tones to offset the more dominant yellow and red shades of wallflowers. Alternatively, both *Bellis* and pansies make good groundwork for the shorter-stemmed tulips in the smaller beds. The *Fosteriana* hybrids and the early single

Left:
'Royal Blue' forget-me-nots filtering through the wallflowers make a suitable 'base coat' for the deep maroon of 'Giant' and the creamy-yellow of 'Niphetos' Darwin tulips.
Below:
The brilliance of Darwin tulip 'Charles Needham' is softened by the pastel chamois-rose of wallflower 'Eastern Queen' and the forget-me-nots.

tulips are the best companions for primroses and for *Primula denticulata*; the Triumph tulips blend well with polyanthus; the Darwin, Cottage, lily-flowered and other tall, late-blooming tulips are best for wallflower associations, and the dwarfer varieties of these together with the early double tulips look attractive over a ground-coat of pansies, *Bellis* or dwarf *Myosotis*. Purple and mauve tulips are particularly effective over yellow, primrose or white wallflowers. Separate varieties or a mixture of two to harmonise with

the groundwork are always more pleasing than full mixtures.

The more thought devoted to the initial planning of flower beds and borders, the more satisfying will be the finished result: a mere conglomeration of different plant colours and shapes can rarely be as pleasing in a garden as the beautiful, well-balanced picture that will emerge when the relationships of one plant to another have been thought out with care and sensitivity. Very little extra effort is needed – and the results will be infinitely more rewarding.

Above:
A delicate combination of tulips 'Smiling Queen' and 'Northern Queen', with pink and white daisies inter-planted with *Myosotis* 'Dwarf Royal Blue'.
Right:
Pomponette daisies with *Myosotis* 'Dwarf Royal Blue' make a charming picture in a small bed or used to furnish a corner.

Index